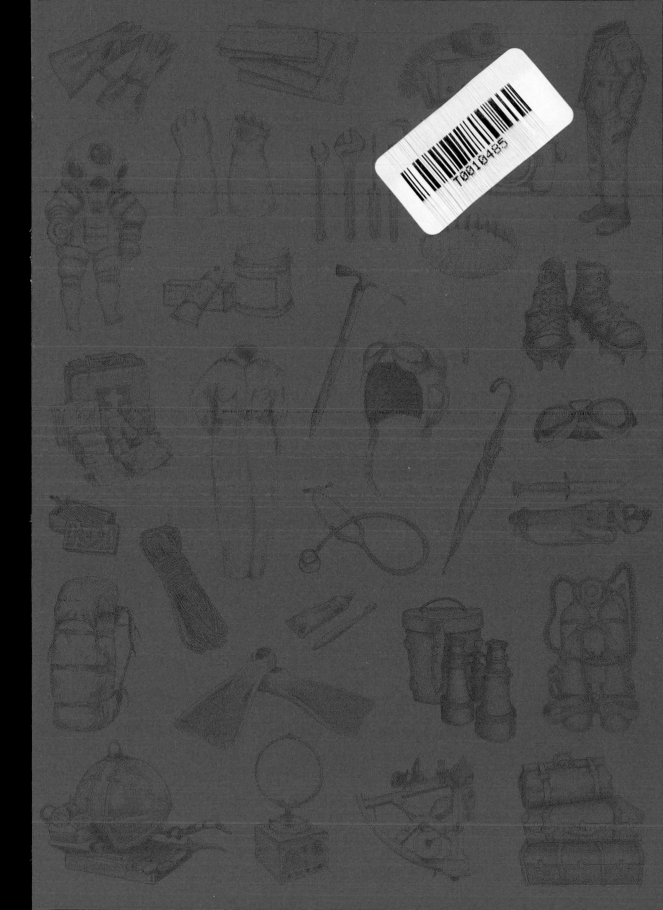

WE ARE
EXPLORERS

WE ARE EXPLORERS

Extraordinary women who discovered the world

Stories and illustrations by

Kari Herbert

Contents

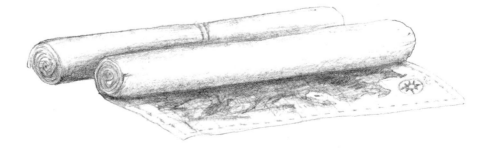

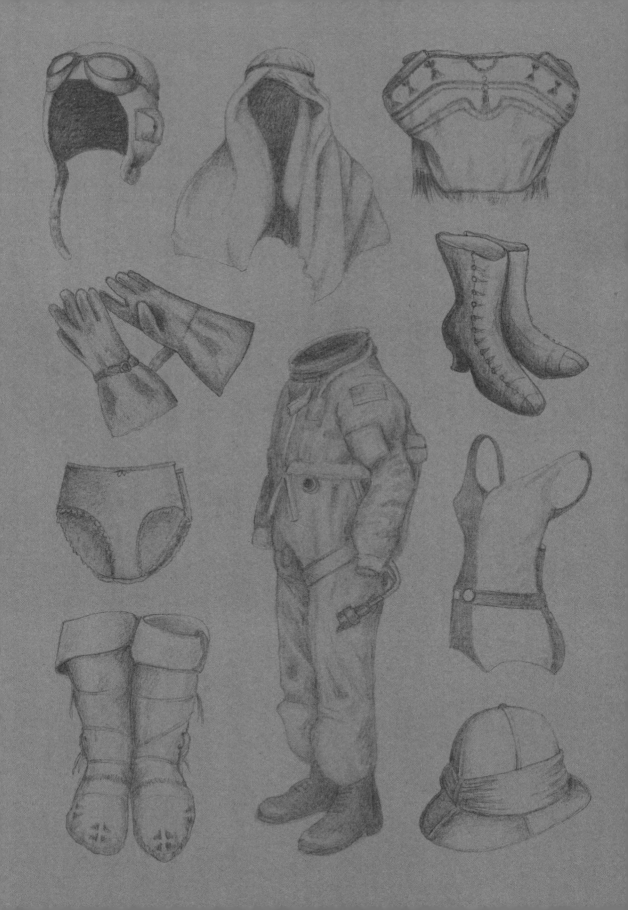

WE ARE EXPLORERS

MANIFESTO

So, you want to be an EXPLORER?

Be curious.
Ask questions, but search for the answers yourself.

Make a plan.
Take a map, but be willing to go beyond it.

Be brave.
You don't need to go far, you just need to go well.

Keep your eyes open.
Make every step an adventure.

Find a new path. Find *your* path.

Most importantly:
make sure you come home to share your story.

Introduction

This book celebrates fourteen awesome explorers who traveled to the farthest reaches of the world. In their stories we journey deep into the desert and rainforest. We discover ancient ruins and fabled cities, climb huge mountain ranges, and canoe down wild rivers. We dive deep in the ocean and soar into space. These are some of the world's most remarkable adventurers. They also all happen to be women.

Women have been journeying for thousands of years. They have explored almost every corner of the globe. Yet, until recently, exploration has been seen as a male-only pursuit. Explorers in this book made important discoveries. But no matter how impressive their achievements, many were dismissed as reckless or eccentric. Some were simply ignored. Who knows how many intrepid women have been forgotten or how many stories of indigenous wayfarers, sailors or guides have been lost to history, as there is no written record to remember them by. This book aims to give voice to at least a few of these extraordinary individuals.

Exploration usually requires money. One hundred years ago the majority of women were not allowed to vote, let alone take control of their own wallets. Those fortunate few who were independently wealthy were not expected to take off alone around the world. Lucky for us some did and they radically redefined women's roles in society. It was not a single effort, but one that happened gradually and collectively.

Real exploration is not about people conquering nature or boasting about their achievements—it is about knowledge. A true explorer has an original idea, and contributes something meaningful through their journeys. They may encounter a new species, create a map of unexplored territory, unearth clues about ancient civilizations or bring a new awareness of the world in which we live. That's why exploration has never been more important, and why these stories are valuable.

Exploration can be a dangerous business. All the individuals in this book, at some point in their lives, took a risk. They were willing to face danger and embrace the unknown, and all kept going, no matter what. Each has been chosen for her incredible achievements, despite being faced with challenges. Although they were all very different characters, they were all courageous, curious and determined women who challenged the accepted norms.

I hope these stories encourage you to embark on your own journeys. They need not be perilous! Many of the women in this book began by first exploring the area in which they lived. You don't have to go far to have an adventure. Simply open your eyes to the world. There is so much still to be discovered.

Kari Herbert

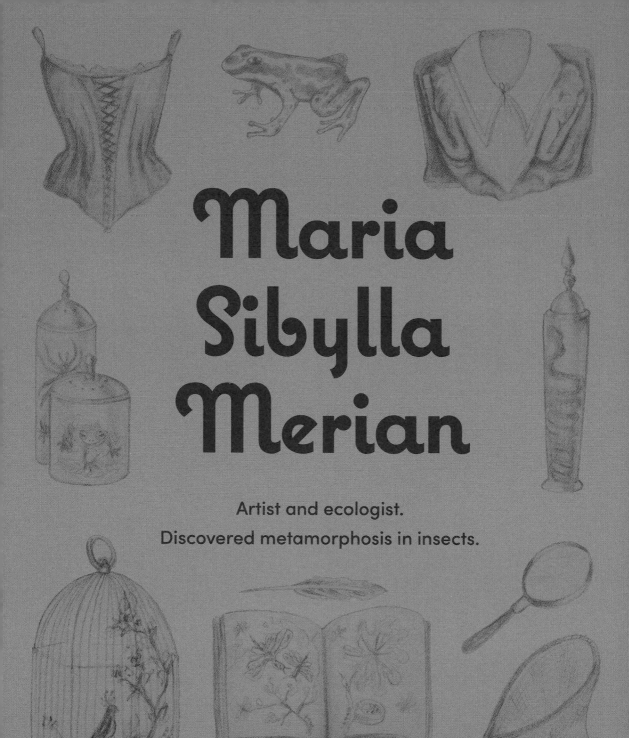

Maria Sibylla Merian

Artist and ecologist.
Discovered metamorphosis in insects.

Maria Sibylla Merian
Miraculous Creatures

The heat was deep and intense. The air was so heavy with moisture that it was difficult to breathe. A glimpse of coral-pink beyond the undergrowth revealed itself to be a flock of scarlet ibis picking their way through tangled mangrove roots. Sounds swirled around her: the drone of frogs and insects, the calls of tropical birds, the whoops of howler monkeys. It had never occurred to her that the jungles of Suriname would be so noisy, or feel so alive. She rested her hand on a branch. There, edging towards her fingers, was the biggest caterpillar she had ever seen. She placed it gently on some leaves in one of her wooden boxes. She had come a long way to find specimens like this. "You are beautiful," she whispered. "I wonder what you will become."

Maria Sibylla Merian had been fascinated by bugs and butterflies for as long as she could remember. They were miraculous creatures, she thought, mysterious too. When she was a child, most of the people where she lived knew nothing about them.

Tropical wildlife. This rainbow whiptail lizard made its home in Maria's house in Suriname. Her paintings showed plants, insects and fruit, like the banana, that had rarely been seen in Europe.

In 1650s Germany, people Maria knew believed that insects grew from dead things or dung. Some thought they were evil. One of the few insects whose life cycle was understood and not deemed "evil" was the silkworm, which spun shimmering threads around itself to make a cocoon. These threads were used to produce luxurious fabric. Maria was intrigued.

As a young girl, Maria was certain that there was a connection between caterpillars and butterflies, but the only way to prove it was to observe and draw the stages of their transformation, or "metamorphosis," from egg to caterpillar to butterfly. Maria obtained a few silkworms, then sat down and watched. Eventually, some began to spin their cocoons. Weeks later, they emerged as beautiful silk moths, fluttering their soft, crumpled wings. She drew and recorded every detail.

Art was Maria's family business. Her father had run a successful publishing shop and when he died, Maria's mother, Johanna, married the artist and engraver Jacob Marrel. He encouraged Maria's talent for drawing and taught her everything he knew. When she turned eighteen, Maria married the artist Johann Andreas Graff. Soon she was a mother. But she was a businesswoman and artist, too. She ran her own successful studio, employing young women artists and selling art supplies and hand-painted silks with her own flower designs.

Curious creatures. An engraving of eggs, caterpillars and butterflies from Maria's book *Metamorphosis Insectorum Surinamensium*.

Fiercely independent, Maria eventually decided to divorce her husband and move to Amsterdam in the Netherlands. There she met merchants and wealthy collectors who told her stories of wild places, brimming with exotic plants and insects. Maria longed to study and paint these marvelous creatures in their natural habitat, so she decided to mount the first scientific expedition to Suriname, a Dutch colony in the jungles of present-day Guyana, South America.

It was a bold plan. The jungle was impenetrable, she was told. Even if she managed to hack a way in, she would encounter deadly snakes and spiders, and find the heat and humidity intolerable. Any expedition there would be doomed to failure. No one was willing to pay for a woman's expedition, but Maria was undaunted. She sold over 250 paintings and her collection of butterflies to raise the money she needed. Then she wrote her will and filled crates with art materials, magnifying glasses and specimen jars.

In 1699, after two uncomfortable months at sea, Maria and her youngest daughter, Dorothea, arrived in Suriname. How different it was to Amsterdam! Papayas, guavas, and bananas grew everywhere. Maria tried pineapple for the first time. Its fragrance, she noted in delight, could fill a room.

Wrestling with nature. Maria and her daughter Dorothea often painted together. This depiction of a caiman wrestling a coral snake expresses the drama in nature.

The tropics were bewildering. Trees soared upwards, over 100 feet high. Some butterflies were larger and faster than birds! The colors were dazzling. Everywhere she looked there seemed to be some miracle of nature. A blue lizard laid eggs inside her home, hummingbirds and butterflies filled her garden. But harmless-looking creatures here could be dangerous. Some frogs and caterpillars were even poisonous.

Indigenous Arawak women showed Maria and Dorothea how things were done. They spun cotton for the hammocks on which they slept, baked bread on banana leaves and taught Maria which herbs and plants could be used as medicines. They brought her caterpillars and maggots to study, too.

For two years Maria and her daughter gathered specimens in Suriname and observed them as they underwent their mysterious transformations. "The heat in this country is staggering," she wrote to a friend, "so that one can do no work at all without great difficulty." Suffering with fever and exhaustion, Maria returned home in 1701.

Naturalists and collectors were excited to see what marvels Maria had brought back from South America. There were caterpillars that she had kept alive during the voyage home, and creatures that she had preserved in jars of alcohol, such as snakes, lantern flies, and even a crocodile. She had to bring them home simply to prove that they really did exist!

In 1705, Maria began creating her book *Metamorphosis Insectorum Surinamensium*. Each painting within opened into its own ecosystem, so vividly colored and highly detailed that it seemed the tarantulas or frogs could crawl off the page.

Maria was one of the early pioneers of ecology. She changed the way artists depicted certain aspects of nature, and dared naturalists to look more closely at the relationships between plants and animals. She challenged the superstition that leaves turned into moths, or that toads sprung, fully formed, from mud. But her greatest legacy, perhaps, was to remind us to appreciate the smallest of beings, and, most of all, never to underestimate girls who collect caterpillars.

Exotic fruit. One of the joys of exploring Suriname was discovering its delicious fruit. Pineapples were Maria's favorite.

Jeanne Baret

Sailor and botanist.
Collected rare plant species.

Jeanne Baret

Hidden Identity

It was a cold December night in 1766. The streets of the French port of Rochefort were dark, save for the dim glow of lamplight escaping from shuttered windows. The young woman crept towards the harbor. She tugged her red cap down over her brow and pulled the thick coat around her. Passersby would likely imagine she was just an ordinary young sailor. But this young woman intended to live a life far from ordinary. Disguised as a man, she intended to board a ship which was about to sail around the world.

Jeanne Baret mumbled the password at the entrance to the dock and climbed aboard, only to find herself face-to-face with a crowd of officers. Asked to identify herself, she boldly answered that she was Monsieur Jean Baret, assistant and valet to Philibert Commerçon, the expedition's naturalist.

As a young girl, Jeanne had been taught by the women in her family in the Loire Valley, France, to make medicines from the roots, flowers, berries, and leaves of wild plants. Even though Commerçon was a famous naturalist, he knew that the knowledge of herb women like Jeanne could be invaluable. Jeanne became his teacher, his housekeeper, his nurse and his assistant. With their shared love of the natural world, it was not long before they were inseparable.

In 1765, Commerçon was invited to participate in the first French scientific circumnavigation of the world, led by the celebrated navigator, Louis Antoine de Bougainville on the ships *Boudeuse* and *Étoile*. It would be one of the greatest voyages of the time, but Commerçon hesitated. It was unthinkable to join this expedition without Jeanne, but women were strictly prohibited from sailing on naval vessels. The couple came up with a daring scheme. Jeanne would join the ship pretending to be his male assistant. It was a risky plan. There was no knowing what would happen to her if her true identity was discovered.

The ships sailed south, hugging the coast of Brazil and Argentina. Along the way, the naturalist and his assistant were put ashore to collect specimens. Commerçon, suffering with leg problems, could not walk far so it was Jeanne who climbed the cliffs and hillsides to select and bring back plants for his collection. She made it her mission to find and record as many new plants as possible, the most famous being the flowery tropical vine that they named after their commander: the Bougainvillea.

The two-year-long voyage was challenging. Every day, Jeanne wrapped linen tightly around her chest to flatten her breasts and keep herself disguised. She endured treacherous seas, feared pirate attacks, and only had the male crew for company. Meals were meager and repetitive: salt-cured pork or beef; hard, stale biscuits; and occasionally fish, if the crew managed to catch any. As they sailed across the Pacific, the crew began to suffer from scurvy and malnutrition. The sick lay on makeshift beds of old sacking. The smell belowdecks was unbearable and the ship became infested with rats, which often made their way into the cook's soup. "There have been many arguments over where Hell is situated," Bougainville wrote, "truly we have found it."

Herb woman. Jeanne's knowledge of plants and herbs proved invaluable during her voyage around the world.

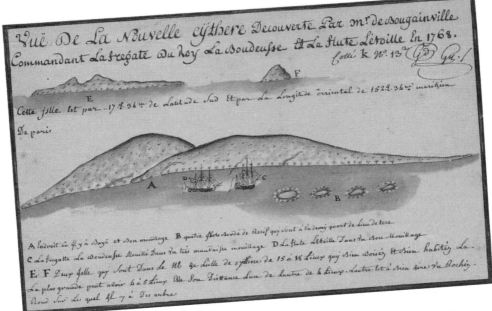

Jeanne's discovery. Drawing of Tahiti.
It was here that Jeanne's disguise was revealed.

Despite all this, Jeanne persisted. She succeeded in crossing the highest mountains of the Strait of Magellan in southern Chile, and explored the deepest forests of the South Pacific islands to build an extraordinary collection of new plant specimens. She worked tirelessly, carrying all the boxes of specimens and scientific equipment herself without complaint, no matter how heavy or cumbersome. But eventually, her secret unraveled.

In April 1768, the ships lay at anchor off the coast of Tahiti. According to Bougainville, Jeanne was ashore to collect specimens, but as she crossed the beach the local Tahitian men saw through her disguise. Scared, she called out for help. It was only then that her French compatriots realized that for well over a year a woman had been living among them.

Bougainville allowed Jeanne to remain onboard until they reached Mauritius, an Indian Ocean island, where Commerçon had been offered a position at the Botanic Garden. Five years later, in 1773, Commerçon died. Jeanne eventually secured a passage back to France in 1775, and became the first woman to have completed a circumnavigation of the globe. In recognition of her dedication and hard work, her old commander, Bougainville, ensured that she would receive a full naval pension—an honor reserved only for men. "This extraordinary woman," as he called her, lived the rest of her days in comfort as a tavern-keeper.

Jeanne's achievements are only truly being recognized now as those of a seventeenth-century woman from a working-class background, who dared to defy the rules and circle the world for the love of plants. Even today, we do not know precisely how many new species she discovered because of the 6,000 plant specimens they collected together, all are attributed to Commerçon. But Jeanne would be content to know that in 2012 a newly discovered climbing plant was named *Solanum baretiae* in her honor.

Sacagawea

Guide and interpreter.
Part of the Lewis and Clark Expedition.

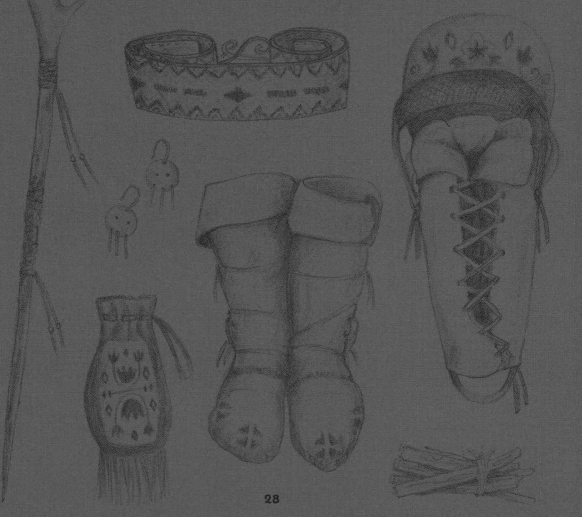

Sacagawea
A Safe Passage

The canoes hurtled down through the rapids. Sacagawea knelt at the front, one hand gripping the side, the other holding her baby tightly to her chest. She shouted directions over the roar of the river to the men, who paddled desperately between the jagged rocks looming either side. None of them saw the wave until it was on top of them. Boxes containing the maps and journals of the expedition were swept away. The men stared at the river in horror. Quickly, Sacagawea handed her baby to her husband and plunged into the river. When she re-emerged, her arms were filled with the expedition's most precious items. It would not be the last time she would save the day.

Sacagawea was born to the Lemhi Shoshone tribe in the forests of what are now known as the Bitterroot Mountains in present-day Idaho. She learned how to live off the land and felt safe and loved with her people. But, when she was twelve, her tribe was attacked by a war party of Hidatsa people. Sacagawea was captured and taken to a settlement at Knife River in present-day North Dakota. There she was sold to Toussaint Charbonneau, a fur trader, who took Sacagawea as his wife. She was sixteen when she became pregnant.

Leading the way. Painting of Sacagawea guiding Lewis and Clark on their journey across North America.

The first time that Sacagawea—"Sah-kah-ga-wi-ah," meaning Bird Woman—saw a white person was when the Corps of Discovery expedition arrived at Knife River in 1804. The Native Americans had lived there for thousands of years. But to white settlers, the area where Sacagawea was born, stretching from what they knew as the Mississippi River to the Rocky Mountains, was a mystery. Many believed that this uncharted wilderness was filled with woolly mammoths and giant sloths. President Thomas Jefferson tasked Captains Meriwether Lewis and William Clark to report on what was there and find a safe route to the Pacific Ocean.

The Corps of Discovery needed local guides to help them. Lewis and Clark agreed to hire Charbonneau if Sacagawea came along too. They needed a Shoshone interpreter to help trade for horses once they reached the mountains. They knew too that she would prove that they were a peaceful expedition—for practical reasons, a war party would not travel with a woman and child.

Together they paddled up the Missouri River, Sacagawea carrying her two-month-old son on her back. For these men it would be a journey into the unknown. For her it was a homecoming: a return to the land from which she'd been taken.

Uncharted ground. Sacagawea helped negotiate a peaceful passage for the explorers through different tribal lands.

For months the party traveled west, battling torrents of water, or hauling their boats and equipment around waterfalls only to come face-to-face with grizzly bears. Their moccasins became shredded by thorny bushes until their feet bled. Sacagawea grew so ill the men thought she would die. But she was determined to keep herself alive for the sake of her baby.

In August 1805, the party met a group of Shoshones. Their Chief was Sacagawea's brother. It had been five years since they had seen each other. For his sister, Chief Cameahwait agreed to provide the horses they needed. Instead of staying with her family, Sacagawea chose to continue. Ahead was a 140-mile trek across the ice-covered Bitterroots, but now she was determined to see the great waters of the Pacific, no matter what.

Blizzards chilled them to their bones as they staggered through thigh-deep snow. Their food ran out. Soon they were reduced to eating candles to survive. Weak, cold, and still nursing her baby, Sacagawea dug for nutritious roots to help the group regain their strength. As they neared the Pacific, the captains held a vote to decide where to settle for the winter. Sacagawea was counted as equal to the other men. It was the first time that a woman had been allowed to participate in a vote sanctioned by the U.S. government, proving how vital she was to the expedition.

Sacagawea helped guide a safe passage as the Corps traveled thousands of miles through the territories of many Native American tribes. She knew where to find food when hunting was scarce and helped the captains identify over 300 species of plants and animals. Yet, when the expedition finished in August 1806, Charbonneau was paid and given land, but Sacagawea received nothing.

Six years after the expedition, Sacagawea became ill and died. She was just twenty-five. Although Lewis and Clark had named a river for her, it was only much later that her contribution was fully recognized. Sacagawea was taken from her home and mistreated, but her determination to see beyond the horizon kept her going. Her story is now inspiring a new generation, reminding others to be strong and keep going, no matter what.

Celebrating adventure. Sacagawea was featured on a United States postage stamp in 1954, and in 2000 on a commemorative coin.

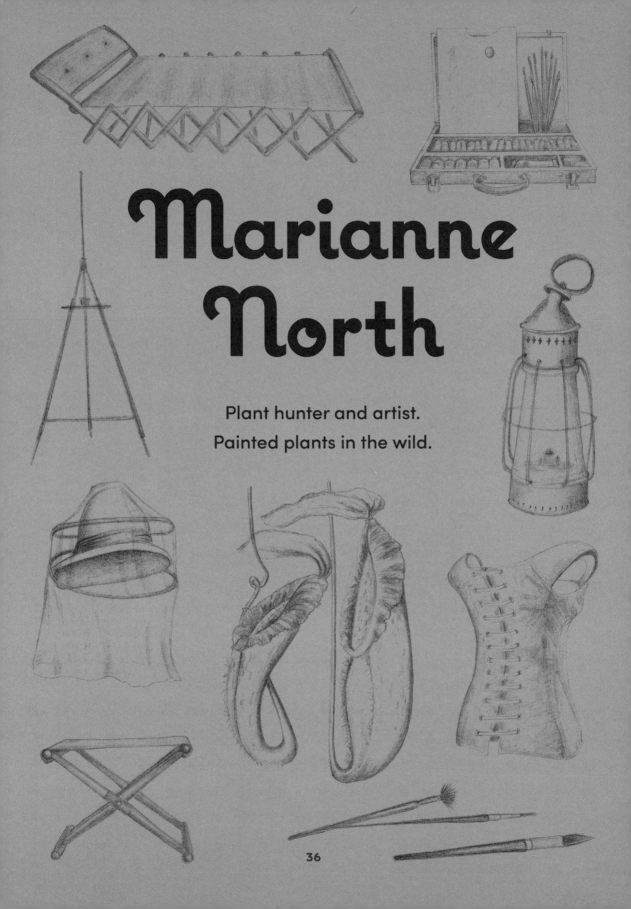

Marianne North

Plant hunter and artist.
Painted plants in the wild.

Marianne North

Growing Wild

When the narrow mountain track became too steep they tied up the horses and continued on foot. Soon they were lost in cloud. Marianne could not see her hand in front of her face. Ahead, strange shapes loomed through the mist—Blue Puya—flowers she had trekked so far to find. At last, beams of sunlight brought the flowers to life in all their color and beauty. This, she thought, is what happiness feels like.

Marianne North was born in Hastings, England. After her mother died, Marianne and her father spent many years traveling. They visited Egypt and Syria and toured Europe. When home, their explorations continued as they learned more about new species of plants at the Royal Botanic Gardens at Kew.

Blue Puya. Marianne's oil paintings showed unusual plants in their natural setting, like this Blue Puya in Chile.

Then her beloved father died, too. Aged forty-one, wealthy and unmarried, she decided to become her own style of plant explorer. Growing up she had been trained in painting. Now, instead of pulling up plants as specimens she would create a visual record of them in their natural environment.

First, she traveled to Canada and the United States. Then, in Jamaica she lived within the old deserted Botanic Gardens surrounded by tangles of orchids and passion flowers, gigantic breadfruit and mangoes. Brazil was next. For eight months she lived in a hut deep in the forest, painting the wild flora around her.

Marianne knew many influential people: scientists, botanists, writers, artists and politicians. Carrying their letters of introduction, she was invited to stay with diplomats and royal families. She appreciated their hospitality, but preferred the company of plants: "I am a very wild bird and like liberty," she would explain, before heading into the bush.

Marianne's travel writings were not always an easy read. She believed she was superior to the indigenous peoples she encountered on her travels and was often critical of their culture. Marianne devoted her life to recording the rich diversity of nature, and it's just a pity that she, like many colonial travelers of her time, did not take care to understand the wondrous variety of human culture too.

Every day she searched for unusual flora, traveling by bullock cart, dugout canoe or on horseback. Sometimes a mule ride became a week-long trek through torrential rains and knee-high mud. The jungle was alive with mosquitoes and leeches, spiders as big as sparrows and apes that followed her through the trees. Always she painted, even when ants crawled over her canvas.

Exploring art. Marianne paints at her easel in South Africa, 1883.

Marianne returned home but never stayed long. She began a journey around the world. She climbed volcanoes in Tenerife, painted towering redwoods in California then sailed to Japan, Hong Kong and Vietnam. In Singapore she shrieked with delight at finding wild pitcher plants. Borneo, Java and Ceylon—present-day Sri Lanka—came next, then a year-long tour of India. Marianne had barely returned home when Charles Darwin, the great naturalist, suggested she investigate the flora of Australia and New Zealand. She sailed immediately and went on to Tasmania, South Africa and the Seychelles.

Growing by the day, the collection of images that Marianne created needed a home. With the permission of the Director of the Royal Botanic Gardens, her friend Sir Joseph Hooker, she built her own pavilion at Kew. Marianne's 832 paintings of plants, scenery, birds and insects not only provided a visual tour of the world, they are now also a vital historical record. Many of the species in her artworks have become extinct.

Marianne circled the globe twice. She ventured north and south in her mission to paint the extraordinary variety of plant life on our planet and contributed to a wider appreciation of the natural world. Today, her paintings remind us to take time to marvel at each of nature's wonders, and preserve them as best we can.

Wondrous nature. Marianne explored the mountains of Sarawak in Malaysia to find and paint these peculiar pitcher plants.

Isabella Bird

Photographer and travel writer.
Traveled extensively
around the globe.

Isabella Bird
Cured by Adventure

Snow lifted from the ground and swirled in strange ghostly shapes. Isabella clutched at her hat with one frozen hand, the other holding the reins. The wind grew stronger, stinging with ice. Her eyes froze shut. Stubbornly, she urged her mule forward even though she could not see. The hiss of the blizzard became a roar. Twenty-two hours later, villagers lifted her, half-dead, from her mule. It took two hours for the warmth to return to her body, but she had survived where others had not. Five men caught in the same blizzard had died.

As a child, Isabella suffered from a spinal disease of which there seemed no cure. Home life in Yorkshire in the 1830s left her feeling trapped by her body. It was a summer in the Scottish Highlands that changed everything. The wide open spaces gave her strength. She leaped over mountain streams and scrambled up hillsides. Coming home, her illness quickly returned. Clearly what she needed, a doctor advised, was a long sea voyage.

Pioneer pony. An illustration of Isabella's riding kit and pony Birdie, from her book *A Lady's Life in the Rocky Mountains*.

With her health as an excuse, she embarked on a life of adventure. Aged twenty-three, Isabella set out for North America. She traveled over 5,500 miles in six months through Canada and the U.S. but as soon as she came home she fell ill again.

Exploration restored her health and became her reason for living. At forty-one years old, her travels took her to California. Here she met the notorious ruffian, "Rocky Mountain Jim." Together they trekked into the wilderness. Isabella was tough. She could round up cattle, melt snow in a tin to wash by the fire and was even known to have killed rattlesnakes with a kitchen knife. She would ride for twelve hours through snowdrifts without complaint then would sleep on the ground, using pine shoots for a mattress and her Mexican saddle as a pillow. Her traveling life was simple but adventurous, and she loved it.

When her beloved sister Henrietta became incurably ill, Isabella returned to England, eventually marrying her sister's doctor. When Isabella's husband also died, she refused to grieve at home. She studied medicine and photography and, aged sixty, set off for India and then East Asia. Photography was her new passion. Now, as well as writing, she photographed the places and people she encountered.

No matter how challenging her surroundings, or how heavy her photographic equipment, Isabella kept to her task. She even developed her own negatives on remote mountain trails and on simple houseboats on the Yangtze River in China.

On the Yangtze. Photo taken by Isabella of her houseboat in China, 1895.

It is remarkable how much Isabella endured on her travels, given her poor health whenever she was at home. She survived blizzards, suffered a broken rib falling into a stream, a broken arm in a cart accident, and was pelted with stones by villagers who distrusted foreigners. But traveling through remote regions also had great rewards. She lived happily with the Ainu tribe on the island of Hokkaido, Japan; navigated the awe-inspiring gorges of the Yangtze; discovered untamed subtropical forests in China; and rode an elephant in Malaysia. At seventy, she rode a gleaming black horse for 680 miles through Morocco. When she died in Edinburgh in 1904, her luggage and cameras were packed and ready for one last trip to China.

Gods and temples. Glass slides of Isabella's photos were hand-colored for her talks.

Isabella at her desk. Isabella's books about her travels became hugely popular, making her a household name.

Isabella wrote many books about her experiences and created an extraordinary photographic archive of places few westerners had ever seen. A popular speaker, she could draw crowds of up to two thousand to her lectures. She was the first woman to become a fellow of the Royal Scottish Geographical Society and the prestigious Royal Geographical Society in London, breaking the barrier for women to be accepted as explorers in their own right. Just as importantly, Isabella demonstrated that physical limitations should not prevent anyone from leading an extraordinary, adventurous life.

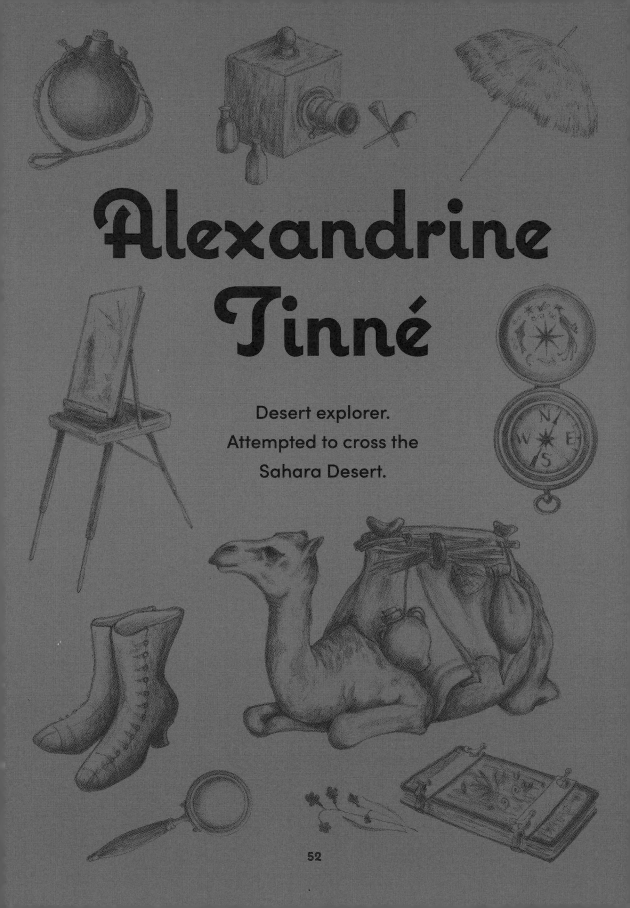

Alexandrine Tinné

Desert explorer.
Attempted to cross the
Sahara Desert.

Alexandrine Tinné

In the Face of Difficulty

Dawn broke over the Nile River. The nighttime roaring of hippos was replaced by birdsong. Alexine frowned. Ahead, the river was choked with ambatch, floating forests of marsh trees. The expedition tried hacking at the vegetation, but the river was impassable. Alexine would not accept defeat. She laid out a map in her cabin and studied it carefully, then called for the captain. If they could go no further by boat, they would explore on foot.

Alexandrine Tinné, known as Alexine, was born into one of Holland's most respected families. The Tinnés were adventurous and free-thinking. As a child Alexine had toured much of Europe with her parents. When her father died, she and her mother, Henriette, continued to travel, visiting Scandinavia then Egypt. They trekked by camel and donkey to the Red Sea, then visited the Holy Land in the Middle East, Syria and Lebanon—places that many at home considered unsafe for women traveling alone.

Lady traveler. An oil painting imagining Alexine riding sidesaddle on one of her adventures.

These adventures were not enough for Alexine. In 1857, at age twenty-two, she sailed up the Nile, reaching as far as Wadi Halfa in Sudan. Some of the greatest explorers of the day—David Livingstone, Richard Burton and John Speke—were all competing to discover the source of the Nile. Ambitious and independently wealthy, Alexine now decided to mount her own expedition to see how far west the Nile basin extended and to try to discover the source herself.

This time she was accompanied by both her mother and her Aunt Addy, and a large entourage of Arab crewmen and soldiers. It was dangerous territory they were entering, overrun with tropical diseases, warring tribes and slave traders. No Europeans, and certainly no women, had explored further than Gondokoro island in southern Sudan, but Alexine and her family were undeterred.

Explorers' journals. Alexine filled sketchbooks with watercolors of her experiences, such as this view of an island near Khartoum and her desert camp.

They spent a year in the region, sailing farther up the White Nile than any European women before. They marveled at hippos, elephants, giraffes and ostriches, photographing and recording anything they thought might be useful to future explorers. Then news reached them that Speke had discovered the source of the Nile. Instead of quitting, Alexine decided to navigate up the marshlands of Bahr el-Ghazal, a tributary of the Nile, then explore overland in search of a great lake which was rumored to exist in Central Africa.

Months of heavy rain made it impossible to continue. The adventure turned into a nightmare. Their tents collapsed under ferocious rainstorms and the party became desperately ill. Alexine's mother and aunt died. Alexine survived, but her world had fallen apart. She blamed herself for the deaths of those she loved most. Too heartbroken to return home, she instead moved to Cairo. There, she created a refuge for freed slaves, then traveled into Algeria, Tunisia and other parts of the Mediterranean.

Despite the terrible failure of her last expedition, Alexine was captivated by the desert. In 1869 she set out from Tripoli in Libya, determined to become the first Western woman to cross the Sahara Desert and perhaps discover the source of the Congo River. Both goals were considered hazardous if not impossible, particularly for a young female explorer.

Alexine understood the harsh desert conditions very well. This time, her caravan of over one hundred camels carried two iron tanks filled with water as well as essential expedition equipment: an easel, canvases and paints, her camera and developing apparatus, an entire library of books, and her botanical and ethnological specimens. News soon spread of the "Blonde Sultaness" riding through the desert. Tuareg tribe people believed that her water tanks were filled with gold. The caravan was raided, and in the confusion Alexine was killed. She was just thirty-three years old.

Young, privileged and female, Alexine's remarkable journeys have now mostly been forgotten. But, she had earned the respect of her fellow explorers. In a memorial, David Livingstone said: "The work of Speke and Grant is deserving of highest commendation ... But none rises higher in my estimation than the Dutch lady, Miss Tinné, who ... nobly persevered in the teeth of every difficulty."

Josephine Peary

Polar traveler.
Explored northern Greenland.

Josephine Peary
Into the Ice

The Arctic storm raged. The blizzard swallowed up the land, sea and sky. Snowflakes became icy darts, stinging exposed faces and hands, and blinding eyes. Josephine Peary had made several journeys to Greenland in the past, but this was her first without her husband by her side. She pulled her daughter close. They were dressed in their warmest furs, ready for the worst. Hours passed, though it seemed like days.

Then there was silence. But they were not safe. During the storm, an enormous iceberg had become wedged across the mouth of the natural harbor where their ship was now stranded. Not even dynamite would move it. The sea began to freeze. They were trapped in one of the most inhospitable places in the world, with no chance of escape.

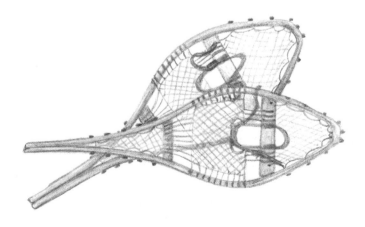

Ship shape. Jo traveled to the Arctic many times with her husband Robert, supporting his attempts to discover the North Pole.

Josephine Diebitsch—known as Jo—was the daughter of Prussian immigrants Hermann von Diebitsch and Magdalena Schmid, a descendant of the German publishing firm Tauchnitz. Jo had studied at a business school in Washington, D.C., and had taken over her father's duties as head clerk of the Smithsonian Institution. When she first met the explorer Robert Peary at a dance, she was impressed. Like her, he was fiery and ambitious, and he dreamed big. Robert had never met a woman so clever and headstrong—he was immediately smitten. Jo agreed to marry him, as long as she could join him on his adventures.

When Robert announced in 1891 that his wife would be accompanying him to the Arctic on a perilous quest it caused an uproar! A woman on an expedition? Preposterous! Some claimed that it was a publicity stunt, others—including Robert's men—claimed that Jo was putting an important expedition at risk. Jo ignored her critics. She would be the first woman to take part in a polar expedition, and she intended to make this adventure as much her own as her husband's.

Just a month into their voyage, a large piece of ice struck the rudder, slamming the iron tiller against Robert, fracturing his leg. For the next few weeks, Jo was the commander of the expedition: issuing orders to the captain and the other men, and selecting the site where their headquarters would be built. This just made some of the team resent her even more.

While her husband forged northwards, Jo took charge of the expedition headquarters. But with no way to contact her family and friends at home, she grew lonely. A few Inuit women lived nearby, but the difference in language and culture made friendships difficult. The Inuit wore animal and bird skins and lived in small stone dwellings or skin tents lit only by simple lamps, fueled by burning animal fat. They were puzzled by her pale skin, her tight bodices and long dresses, and were fascinated by her soap, hairbrush and mirror.

Even harder than the loneliness was the winter, with its five-month-long darkness. Still Jo was undaunted. Carrying her shotgun over her shoulder, she would walk for hours alone through the moonlight to check her traps.

Often it became so cold that her skirts froze stiff. Sometimes she would be disorientated by sudden blizzards or find herself sliding on ice perilously close to a cliff edge, but fresh meat was essential to keep them all healthy. Returning bruised and sore, she would nevertheless return to her explorations a few days later.

Snowshoes. Jo would often trek alone into the wilderness of northern Greenland to find fresh food for the team.

Snow Baby. Jo's daughter Marie Ahnighito was born in the Arctic. Here she is dressed in traditional Inuit furs to stay warm.

Again and again, the Pearys returned to the far north. Jo even gave birth to her daughter Marie on Greenland's shores. The Inuit called Marie "the Snow Baby" for her white skin.

Now that they had a child, Jo mostly organized their expeditions from the U.S.—lecturing, raising money for further explorations, and sending rescue ships north when Robert got into difficulties. Then came the hardest time. Jo became pregnant with their second child just before Robert left again. The baby never met her father. She died when she was just seven months old. Soon after, Jo heard that her husband had lost most of his toes to frostbite and was refusing to come home. Distraught, she decided to bring him back herself.

By now the press knew that Jo was not to be underestimated. "Mrs. Peary," one article declared, "is a woman who will have her way." Her book *My Arctic Journal* had described her extraordinary adventures, and women across the U.S. were celebrating her determination and bravery. Headlines congratulated "the intrepid Mrs. Peary on her mission to rescue her famous Arctic explorer."

Peary promenade. Magazines and newspapers printed illustrated stories about the Pearys' adventures.

In July 1900, Jo and Marie sailed to where Peary should have been. But a note nailed to the door of the hut simply said, "Gone farther north." Jo urged the captain to keep going, but then came the storm. They were trapped for the winter in one of the bleakest places in the Arctic. Here, many explorers had perished. For the sake of her daughter and the ship's crew, Jo tried to remain in good spirits, despite the ever-present danger, darkness and hardship. Years later, Marie remembered tears rolling down her mother's face as she sang lullabies to soothe her to sleep.

As soon as the light of spring returned, Jo sent Inuit hunters north to find her husband. She and Marie had been marooned for eight long, desperate months before the family was reunited. Eventually, the ice melted and the iceberg that had trapped them drifted away. Despite all they had gone through to bring him home, Robert declared he would stay in the north. Now he had Jo's fresh supplies, he was determined to keep exploring. Heartbroken, Jo and Marie sailed back to the U.S. alone.

Base camp. Jo and Marie were stranded in a desolate part of the Arctic in the winter of 1900.

In 1909, Robert declared he had reached the North Pole. Simultaneously, another explorer, Dr. Frederick Cook, claimed that he was first. Newspapers around the world printed stories on the battle. Eventually, Cook was discredited and Robert was celebrated as the victor. Today, it is generally accepted that Robert miscalculated his position and did not reach the Pole after all. Despite this, the Pearys' achievements were remarkable, and Jo's contribution was vital to both Robert's survival and his success.

Jo proved that a woman could be as valuable on a polar expedition as any man. She brought knowledge of the Inuit culture to a new audience and was granted the National Geographic Society's highest honor—the Medal of Achievement—for her Arctic accomplishments and bravery.

Nellie Bly

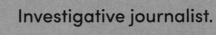

Investigative journalist.
Traveled around the world in 72 days.

Nellie Bly
Race Against Time

The ship's horn blasted through the grand buildings of New York City, drowning out the cheers from the crowd below. A slim figure stood at the ship's rail, dressed in a distinctive long plaid coat. It was November 14, 1889 and this twenty-five-year-old reporter had just begun a race against time.

Nellie Bly smiled and waved, but as the steamship moved away from home she felt overwhelmed. The sea started to swell and the ship rolled. Stories of seafarers enduring storms and shipwrecks filled her mind. "Do you get seasick?" someone asked. "She's going around the world!" teased a man as she heaved over the side. The laughter didn't bother her. She would circle the globe in record time and prove that a woman can do anything she puts her mind to.

Nellie Bly was born Elizabeth Jane Cochran in Pennsylvania, but was known as "Pink" for the color she always wore. She was six years old when her father, Judge Michael Cochran, died. By the time Pink was fifteen, the little money her mother had ran out. She could no longer afford to send her daughter to school so Pink had to find work. Options for women with no qualifications were limited in those days. She could either work in a factory or become a nanny.

One day, she read an article in the *Pittsburgh Dispatch* stating that women should get married, stay at home, and stop talking nonsense about having a career. Pink responded with an angry letter to the editor, signing it "Lonely Orphan Girl." To her surprise, the editor was so impressed by her writing that he offered her a job. She should have a pen name, he said. From then on, she would write as Nellie Bly.

Having a pen name was very useful. Nellie was fearless and ambitious, with a fierce sense of right and wrong. She asked bold questions and wrote challenging stories at a time when few newspapers would hire women. Concealing her real identity meant that she could go undercover to expose true stories no journalists had reported on before. She revealed the tough conditions endured by women factory workers and, when she moved to New York, even pretended she had a mental illness so that she could be admitted to a psychiatric hospital. Her eyewitness reports for the *New York World* on the cruel treatment of patients were astonishing. Nellie Bly was pioneering a new style of reporting, now known as investigative journalism.

One Sunday in 1888, Nellie came up with a brilliant idea for a new assignment. She would circle the world in record time! In her day, there were no airplanes and few cars. People traveled by ship, train, or horse-drawn carriage. The only precedent for this journey was that of Phileas Fogg, a fictional character whose imaginary journey took eighty days. Traveling 22,000 miles in eighty days sounded impossible then, but Nellie wanted to do it even faster.

Her editor at the *World* shook his head when she told him of her plan, telling her that no one but a man could achieve it. "Very well," she replied. "Start the man and I'll start the same day for some other newspaper, and beat him." "I believe you would," he answered thoughtfully.

A year later he called her back into his office and asked, "Can you start around the world the day after tomorrow?" Nellie did not waste a minute. She bought a small satchel in which she could fit only essential things. She had two watches: one of them would be set on New York time for the duration of the trip; the other could be reset for whichever time zone she crossed.

Leaving New York, Nellie sailed for England. From there she made a short detour through France to meet Phileas Fogg's creator, Jules Verne, then headed to Italy and sailed through the Suez Canal in Egypt to Yemen on the Red Sea. Next she traveled to Sri Lanka, Malaysia, Singapore and China.

Seasoned traveler.
Nellie appears in her
traveling outfit after
returning from her
global adventure
in February 1890.

Nellie experienced marvelous things. She toured ancient
cities, rode in rickshaws, tasted spicy curries, and drank tea
with Japanese geishas. She saw towering gold statues of the
Buddha, met merchants selling gleaming jewels, and watched
young boys diving for pearls. In Singapore she even bought a pet
monkey and named it McGinty. Happily, she was finally cured of
seasickness, too.

All the while, thousands of readers followed her progress, eagerly reading the stories she sent back to the *World* by cablegram—a message sent by underwater cables.

Everything seemed to be going to plan, but when she reached Hong Kong, she was greeted with bad news. Another female reporter, Elizabeth Bisland, had been sent around the world by *Cosmopolitan* magazine in an effort to beat Nellie. Worse still, she was already a few days ahead. Nellie was unfazed. "I am not racing with anyone," she said. "I am running a race with Time."

Nellie had less than four weeks to finish her journey. She still had to travel to Japan, and cross both the Pacific Ocean and the American continent to get back to New York. Storms hit her ship and snowstorms buried the train tracks but she pressed on. Elizabeth Bisland was soon left behind.

Nellie's intrepid voyage captured the imagination of the American public. People traveled far and wide to catch a glimpse of her train. They lined the tracks as it steamed past, cheering at the top of their lungs. Nellie had become the most famous woman in the U.S. Thousands of people turned up to greet her as she stepped onto the platform at Jersey City. She took off her cap and whooped. She had traveled around the world in seventy-two days, six hours, eleven minutes and fourteen seconds, setting a world record.

World famous. A newspaper illustration shows the crowds who greeted Nellie on her return home.

Nellie continued to write and champion those who did not have a voice. She got married and ran a large business, but she would always be most famous for her journey around the world. As the mayor of Jersey City had shouted over the screaming crowds as she returned home, "the American girl can no longer be misunderstood! She will be recognized as determined, independent, able to take care of herself wherever she may go."

Alexandra David-Néel

Pilgrim and author.
Journeyed to the Forbidden City of Lhasa.

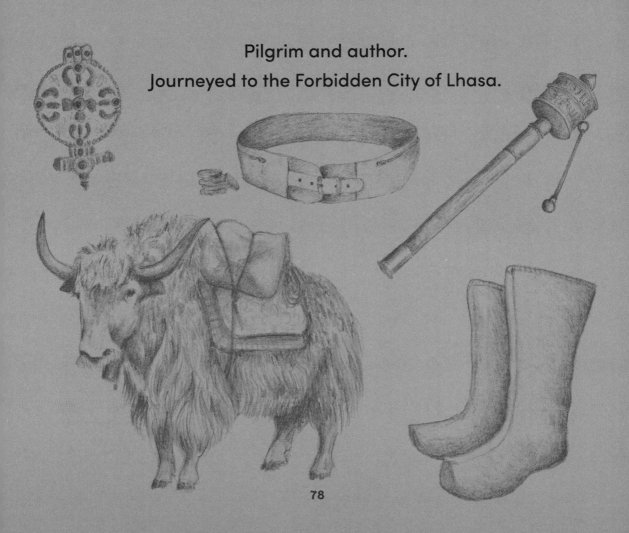

Alexandra David-Néel
A Spiritual Journey

Night had fallen and the high mountain pass was quiet and still. Alexandra gazed at it all, her heart bursting with happiness. Something moved nearby. A snow leopard. Alexandra watched as it padded towards her. She then whispered gently, "You needn't think yourself so special; I have seen a tiger just as close." The snow leopard continued on its way as Alexandra drifted into sleep.

Born in France, but raised in Belgium, Alexandra grew up longing for adventure. From a young age she began running away, once even making it as far as London. At seventeen, clutching only a raincoat and a book of Greek philosophy, she crossed the Swiss Alps alone on foot.

Alexandra was fascinated by Buddhist mythology. She loved to sing, too. While she studied music in Paris, she learned everything she could about Buddhist sacred art, Hindu philosophy and Chinese Taoist philosophy. At age twenty-one she became a Buddhist. Then, at thirty-six, Alexandra made her greatest journey: a fourteen-year voyage through Europe and Asia to the Forbidden City of Lhasa in Tibet.

Traveling companions.
Pictured here in northern Tibet, Alexandra and Yongden would become inseparable.

In 1912, Alexandra traveled to India then Sikkim, a mountainous kingdom in the Himalayas, where she lived in a cave and studied Buddhism. There, she met the Dalai Lama, became a disciple of Gomchen of Lachen, the abbot of a monastery, and befriended the young Lama Aphur Yongden, who would become her lifelong traveling companion and adopted son.

Friends in high places. The Maharaja of Sikkim, Sidkeong Tulku,
and royal companions traveled with Alexandra through Sikkim in 1914.

Together, Alexandra and Yongden traveled through Burma, Bhutan, Japan and Korea, then crossed China by yak, mule and on foot to the Kumbum Monastery on Tibet's doorstep. There, for three years, Alexandra studied ancient texts and learned how to speak Tibetan. She even perfected a difficult yoga technique in which she could raise her body temperature through meditation. It would help her survive the journey across the icy Himalayas.

When it was time to leave for Lhasa, Alexandra and Yongden left behind almost all their possessions; particularly anything a westerner might use, such as a spoon, which would give them away. If Alexandra was discovered, she could be deported, arrested or worse. They would travel as religious pilgrims called *arjopas*. Yongden wore his lama robes, and Alexandra, now nearly fifty, disguised herself as his poor mother. She darkened her face with grease and soot from their cooking pot, colored her hair with ink and added yak-hair braids.

They made traditional tea from river water, butter and salt. They ate *tsampa*—roasted barley flour—sometimes mixed with butter for a treat. With nothing to eat on Christmas Day, they heated snow and made "soup" from boiled scraps of leather from their worn-out boots. If it became too cold or dangerous to sleep, they walked all night. Sometimes robbers armed with knives attempted to steal the few possessions they had. Alexandra would drive them off in a rage.

In January 1924, exhausted and starving, the sight they had been longing to see came into view. Below, at the heart of the Forbidden City, stood the magnificent Potala Palace, the home of the ruling lamas. Alexandra had become the first westerner to cross the Trans-Himalayas in the dead of winter and enter the Forbidden City.

Alexandra's book *My Journey to Lhasa* caused a sensation when it was published in 1927, but more importantly it gave a remarkable record of a place that she had a deep and lasting respect for. Alexandra was an extraordinary woman; an explorer of the world and adventurer of the mind. She continued to travel for the rest of her life and even renewed her passport at age 100! She fully lived her motto: "Go where your heart leads you, where your gaze falls."

Sisters. Alexandra disguised herself as a local pilgrim to enter Tibet. Here she sits with nuns from the Chöten Nyma Monastery in 1914.

Freya Stark

Desert explorer and travel writer.
Re-mapped areas of Iran and Yemen.

Freya Stark

Over Shifting Sands

Heat rippled off the scorched ground. Sand shifted underfoot and flowed over the dunes like smoke. Strange shapes moved silently towards her. Shielding her eyes from the blazing sun, Freya stared in astonishment. Moving towards her were camels. Lots of them. Soon she was surrounded by a herd of five hundred towering animals and their riders. She stood mesmerized. "I never imagined that my first sight of the desert would come with such a shock of beauty," she wrote.

Freya was born in Paris, France, but spent her childhood in England and Italy. Her mother, Flora, was an Italian pianist and her father, Robert, a British artist. Robert encouraged Freya and her sister to be adventurous, and with his constant encouragement she grew up learning to never let fear hold her back.

Camel train. Deep in the Arabian desert, Freya encountered long caravans of traders and camels.

At age thirteen, Freya was involved in a terrifying accident. Her hair became caught in a machine in a rug factory, which scarred her for life. While recovering, she taught herself Latin and read books in French and German. She always had a copy of her favorite book *One Thousand and One Nights* by her side. She dreamed that one day she too would cross the deserts of Arabia and discover lost cities.

When World War I broke out in 1914, Freya volunteered as a nurse at the Italian front, but still she dreamed of the East. Finally, in November 1927, she boarded a cargo ship and headed to Lebanon. It didn't matter to her that the sea was rough, nor that the ship was crammed with pigs—her life of adventure had begun.

Freya was in awe of the formidable explorer Gertrude Bell, known as the Desert Queen, for her bold journeys and influence in the region. Freya wanted to go further.

Traveling light. Freya liked to explore with just a single guide. Here she is in Jabal al-Druze, Syria, in 1928.

She studied maps and spoke with scholars in Beirut, then set out to explore some of the most challenging areas of Iraq, Syria and Lebanon. Ahead of her was searing heat, vast inhospitable land, and territories gripped with political unrest. Despite traveling by night on isolated tracks, she was discovered and charged with being a spy. Freya was chatty and quick to smile whatever the situation. She was released three days later after becoming friends with those who arrested her.

With a single guide, Freya ventured alone from Baghdad, Iraq, to seek the legendary citadel of a medieval prince who sent killers to murder his enemies. Despite suffering dysentery and malaria, she discovered the citadel, charmed tribal leaders and scaled treacherous escarpments without shoes. She returned with new maps, photographs and extraordinary stories. Her informative, entertaining descriptions of her experiences were published in her book *The Valleys of the Assassins,* and would soon make her one of the world's most popular travel writers.

Freya re-mapped Iran's remote Alborz Mountains and located the ancient Arabian port of Cana in Yemen. She followed the route of Alexander the Great and trekked forgotten trade routes through Iraq, Iran, Afghanistan, Samarkand and Soviet Central Asia. In her eighties she rode through Nepal's Annapurna Massif on horseback and voyaged down the Euphrates by raft.

Extreme endeavors. Freya's extraordinary journeys were remembered on a British stamp in 2003.

A world-class explorer and scholar, she received many awards and medals, and in 1972 was named Dame Commander of the British Empire. She lived to be 100 years old.

Freya despaired of those that rush to and from destinations purely to say they have been there. The delight is in the journey itself and how deeply one appreciates every minute. "The genuinely wild soul is not interested in seeing the world, it is interested in being," she said. "It really is how and not what one sees that matters."

Jean Batten

Aviator and record-breaker.
Flew solo from England to New Zealand.

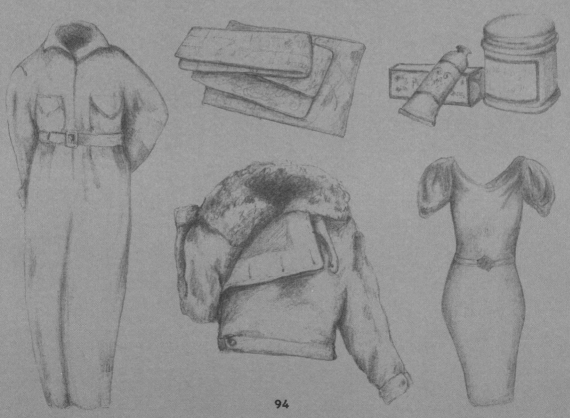

Jean Batten
Flying Solo

The engine of the biplane droned, loud and constant. Suddenly, over Syria, sandstorms struck. The flimsy biplane was thrown about in a whirling nightmare of choking sand, then plummeted downwards. Jean turned off the engine and brought the plane down on a barren desert track. She was cut and bruised, but she was alive. She crawled out of the cockpit, lay down on the sand and drifted into an exhausted sleep.

Jean Batten was born in Rotorua, New Zealand, at a time when flying was the most daring activity on Earth. In the 1910s it was risky and something only men were allowed to do. On weekends, her mother, Nellie, would take her to see the seaplanes at a nearby training school. Jean watched, exhilarated, as the young pilots skimmed their seaplanes just above the water, before lifting into the air. Jean longed to fly with them.

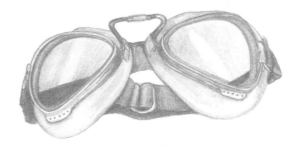

Flying solo. Even as a young girl, Jean longed to fly.
She would become one of the world's greatest aviators.

Jean's mother wrote to the Australian aviator Charles Kingsford Smith, convincing him to teach her daughter how to fly. At age nineteen, Jean was airborne in his plane Southern Cross. Beneath them stretched the Blue Mountains of New South Wales. Rivers became glittering ribbons. Houses were no more than grains of sand scattered over the red earth. "This is it!" she yelled over the roar of the engine. "This is what I have to do!"

In 1930, Jean sailed for London, and joined the London Aeroplane Club, one of the few places where women could train as pilots. As Jean began her training, a fellow club member called Amy Johnson became the first woman aviator, or aviatrix, to fly alone from England to Australia. Jean wanted to fly even further, from England all the way to New Zealand.

No sooner had Jean earned her pilot's licence than she had to go home. Her mother had sold their piano to pay for flying lessons, but the money had run out. Meanwhile, other aviatrixes were setting new records. In 1931, Amy flew from London to Moscow, then across Siberia to Japan, faster than anyone before. In 1932, Amelia Earhart became the first woman to fly solo nonstop across the Atlantic. Long-distance aviators were seen as glamorous daredevils. Jean wanted to be among them. Amy and Amelia had wealthy sponsors. Jean had no money. Yet with charm and persistence, she managed to get hold of a secondhand Gipsy Moth biplane made of wood and fabric. Amy had flown from England to Australia in twenty days. Now Jean planned to make it in fourteen.

On April 9, 1933, Jean's biplane rose into the air and headed south. Jean was used to flying in Britain's gentle weather. Now fog, sandstorms and monsoons forced her to land in places that were dangerous for her fragile aircraft. At one point, she nearly lost her plane to a swamp. Over India, the plane somersaulted and crashed. Miraculously, Jean was unhurt. It took another two attempts before she made it, reaching northern Australia in fourteen days and twenty-two hours. After enjoying her rapturous welcome, she flew back to England, becoming the first aviatrix to make the return flight.

Hero of the skies. Jean stands in her flying suit on the wing of her biplane in 1934.

Jean continued breaking records and, in 1936, achieved her dream of becoming the first to fly solo from England to New Zealand. Thousands gathered to welcome her home. She was an extraordinary pilot, known for both her flying and navigational skills. Using maps, a watch and a compass, she always knew exactly where she was, and where she was going. She received countless honors and became the first woman to win the medal of the Fédération Aéronautique Internationale, aviation's highest honor.

In 1939, though, Jean hung up her flying goggles for good. She lived the rest of her life quietly away from the rest of the world. For this reason, she may not be as well-known as Amy Johnson and Amelia Earhart, but her achievements were as great. Today, a statue of Jean stands outside Auckland Airport, commemorating a woman who captured the imagination of an age, and broke barriers of time, distance and gender.

Welcome home. Jean Batten and guide Bella Papakura greeting each other with a *hongi*, a traditional Māori welcome.

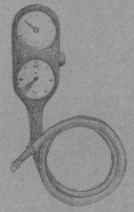

Sylvia Earle

Marine biologist and ocean explorer.
Explored the ocean floor.

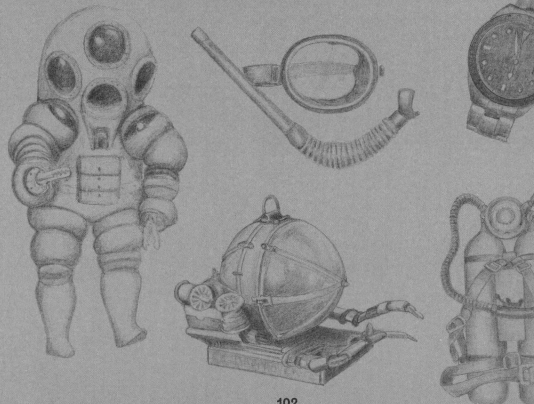

Sylvia Earle
Underwater Life

It was dark at the bottom of the ocean. It was a different kind of dark than you find on land. On land, there is usually a glimmer of moonlight or starlight. This was an inky blackness that was infinitely deep, infinitely mysterious, pierced only by the distant spotlights from the submersible Star II. The beams of light picked out long-legged red crabs swaying on pink coral fans. A shark loomed close, peering at Sylvia before twisting away. A clutch of rays rippled past. Sylvia stepped lightly on the seabed. This was an adventure unlike anything else she had experienced before.

Sylvia grew up on a farm in New Jersey. It had a pond and a creek and an ancient orchard. Sylvia could usually be found by the pond, where every creature and every bloom of algae was recorded in her notebook. When Sylvia was twelve, the family moved to Dunedin, Florida. A few paces away glittered the Gulf of Mexico. Sylvia floated on the surface of the warm waters, gazing at the richness of life beneath.

Aquanaut. This pressurized "Jim" suit enabled Sylvia to breathe while diving very deep underwater.

When she was not in the sea, she was in the library. Her favorite author was William Beebe, an underwater biologist who had explored the ocean depths in the 1920s. Sylvia longed to become a marine biologist but her parents could not afford to send her to college. So Sylvia studied hard, earned scholarships and worked extra jobs to pay for her own education.

In the 1960s, only a few women scientists had the opportunity of working in the field. In 1964, she was invited on a scientific voyage to the Indian Ocean, visiting East Africa, the Seychelles, Kenya, Egypt, Greece and Italy. Her research in marine algae was outstanding and more invitations followed. Now a mother of two with a PhD, she kept exploring. She traveled to the Galápagos, the Chilean Juan Fernández Islands and the Panama Canal Zone.

Sylvia then heard of two revolutionary projects: Man-In-Sea Project and Tektite, in which people would live and work in enclosed underwater habitats on the ocean floor. The plan was as pioneering as space travel. Sylvia was chosen as the leader of a women-only team of aquanauts. In the summer of 1970, Sylvia and her team dove into the waters off the Virgin Islands, and swam down to their new home on the seafloor, making observations and taking photographs of their surroundings.

In the following years, Sylvia traveled the world as chief scientist on expedition after expedition. She followed sperm whales around the globe, explored coral reefs and discovered extraordinary creatures, such as photoblepharon—tiny fish with a bioluminescent spot under each eye.

Then, in September 1979, she traveled to Hawaii to attempt the deepest dive ever made without a cable to the surface. The *Star II* would take Sylvia down 1,250 feet then leave her to explore the seafloor alone. The risks were huge. At that depth the smallest problem could become fatal. If her air supply failed she would suffocate. If the suit sprung a leak, she would be crushed by the tremendous pressure of the ocean above.

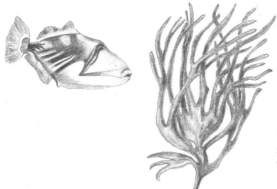

Underwater home. Sylvia below the surface on the Tektite II mission in the Virgin Islands in the summer of 1970.

Far below the surface, Sylvia felt as though she were exploring the surface of the moon. But unlike the moon, here there was life. Sylvia marveled at the sleek lantern fish, and the sparks of living light—bioluminescence—transmitted from tiny transparent creatures that brushed against her faceplate. Alone and untethered, she was exploring the ocean floor deeper than any human being before or since.

Known fondly as "Her Deepness," Sylvia has been at the forefront of ocean exploration for more than four decades, spending thousands of hours underwater. She has pioneered research on marine ecosystems, developed new technologies for undersea and remote exploration, and is a tireless advocate for our oceans. The ocean, Sylvia tells us, is the blue heart of Planet Earth, and we must look after it: "No ocean, no life. No ocean, no us."

Marine marvels. Sylvia investigates a towering tube sponge in Bonaire in the Caribbean.

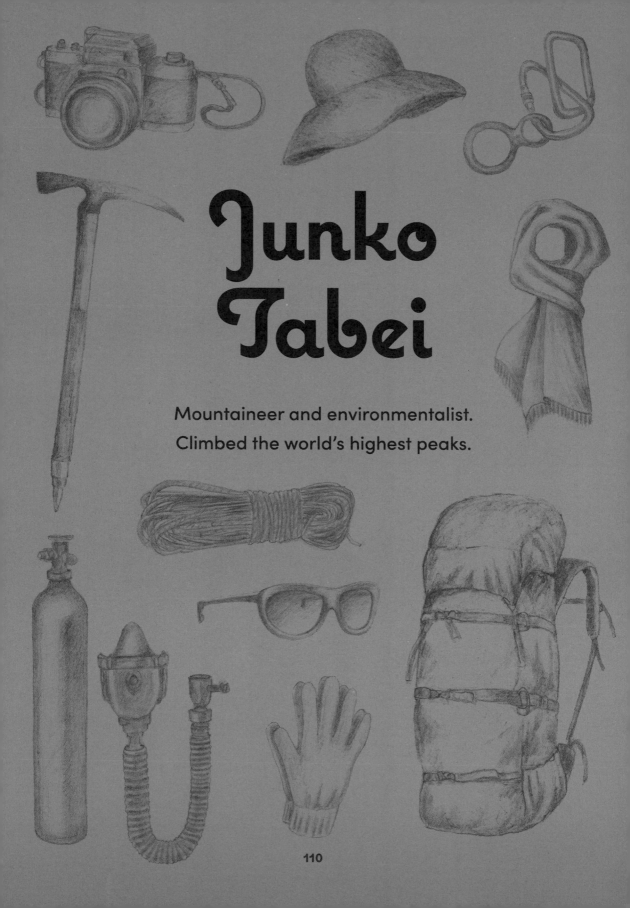

Junko Tabei

Mountaineer and environmentalist.
Climbed the world's highest peaks.

Junko Tabei

Climbing Sky High

The avalanche hit without warning. It was silent and deadly. Within seconds the tent was buried under snow. Junko tried to fight her way out but her arms and legs were tangled in the tent, trapped beneath her four companions. She gasped for air, overwhelmed with fear and frustration. It had taken so much to get here, but now it looked as though she would be frozen forever into Everest's deadly embrace. As hope faded, arms plunged through the snow and pulled her to safety.

Junko's first experience of climbing was at elementary school in Japan, when her class climbed the volcanic Mount Nasu in 1949. She was ten years old. It was like another world on top of the mountain. It was cold despite being summer, yet the mountain stream— fed by a hot spring—was scalding hot. She realized then that there were many remarkable things to experience in nature, and she became determined to explore the world.

Ultimate challenge.
Junko and Sherpa guide
Ang Tshering prepare
to climb Mount Everest
in May 1975.

One of seven children, Junko came from Fukushima, a rural part of Japan where few girls went to high school and hardly any went to college. Junko was an exception. But she felt different from the other students in Tokyo. Her escape was the mountains. Almost every weekend she would go hiking or climbing.

When she graduated, she joined several mountaineering groups looking for opportunities to go on expeditions. By the mid-1960s she had scaled all of Japan's highest mountains, including Mount Fuji. Now she dreamed of going to the Himalayas with a team of women.

Most male climbers were against the idea of women-only expeditions. They laughed at Junko's dream to summit Everest and told her she should find a husband and raise children instead. Junko did marry, then formed the Ladies Climbing Club of Japan and tackled many difficult climbs, including the first women-only ascent to Annapurna III In Nepal. By 1975, at age thirty-five, with a two-year-old daughter at home, Junko was ready to climb Everest.

Climbing the highest mountain in the world was not easy. Only thirty-five mountaineers had so far successfully reached the summit, all guided by Sherpas. When Junko and the Japanese Women's Everest Expedition were hit by an avalanche, they nearly joined the many that had died trying. Thanks to the Sherpas they survived. After the incident, the team were told by the expedition doctor that they should all return to Base Camp. Junko refused. Despite the risk she insisted she go on alone with her guide.

On the summit. Junko becomes the first woman to climb Mount Everest on May 16, 1975.

On May 16, 1975 Junko Tabei and Sherpa Ang Tshering scrambled across a narrow, sharp ridge and stepped foot on the highest point on Earth. The world fell away at their feet. Angular peaks below rose like teeth into the bitter blue sky. Exhausted, and knowing how hard the descent would be, only one thought came to her mind: "Oh, I don't have to climb anymore."

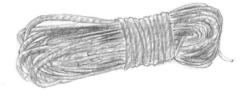

Thoughtful mountaineer. Aware of the increasing impact of climbing tourism, Junko campaigned for the protection of mountain environments.

In 1992, Junko became the first woman to climb the highest peaks on all seven continents, including Kilimanjaro in Tanzania, Denali in Alaska and Vinson in Antarctica. But the more she climbed, the more worried she became about the environmental impact of climbing tourism. The slopes of Everest had become littered with discarded oxygen bottles, broken tents, even the bodies of those who had died en route. At age sixty-one, Junko went back to college to study Environmental Science and became head of the Himalayan Adventure Trust of Japan, dedicated to the protection of mountain environments.

Junko defied the stereotype of a woman's role in her field. Her example would inspire a generation of women mountaineers and adventurers. Her advice to young women was this: "Do not give up. Keep on your quest."

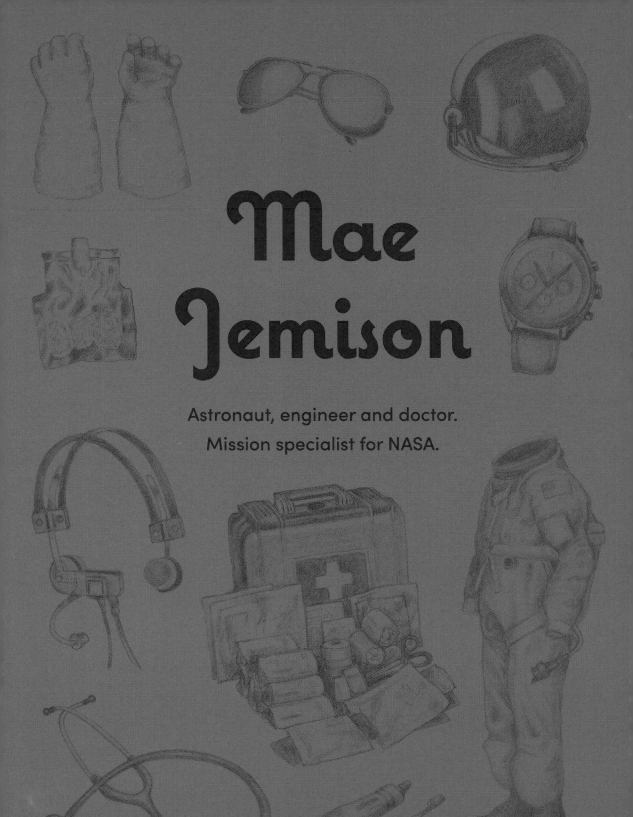

Mae Jemison

Astronaut, engineer and doctor.
Mission specialist for NASA.

Mae Jemison
Universal Connection

The engines ignited. The roar was deafening, drowning out the bleeps of the flight console. Everything rattled. Five ... Four ... Three ... Her heart thumped. Her mind raced. Two ... One ... Lift off! The rocket carrying the space shuttle Endeavour powered upwards. Mae's body was slammed against the seat. Everything was juddering so violently it felt as though the shuttle would be shaken apart. Then they were out of Earth's atmosphere. Everything went quiet and Mae was floating under her harness. She beamed with delight. She had made it to orbit and fulfilled a lifetime's dream.

As a child growing up in the city of Chicago, Mae would often stare up at the stars and wonder what it would be like to travel among them. The universe was huge and complex, there was so much to explore. She wanted to set foot on other planets. Mae imagined that one day she might become a scientist on Mars.

At that time, only one woman had been into space: a Russian cosmonaut called Valentina Tereshkova, who orbited the Earth forty-eight times on a solo mission in the space capsule *Vostok 6* in 1963. In America, though, only white men had been selected for their space program. Mae thought space travel should be more like *Star Trek*, her favorite television show, where all genders and races worked together as the crew aboard the space craft.

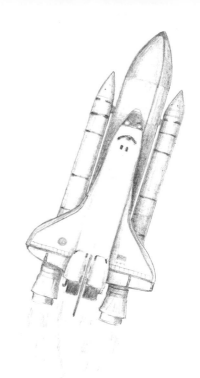

Mae believed she could achieve anything if she worked hard enough. At age sixteen, she won a scholarship to Stanford University to study chemical engineering as well as African and African American studies. She loved dancing too. In her senior year in college she had to decide whether to become a professional dancer or a scientist. She chose science.

Mae studied medicine at Weill Cornell Medical College, but she wanted to see the world. She visited Cuba, traveled to Thailand to work with Cambodian refugees, then worked with flying doctors in East Africa. At age twenty-six, she joined the Peace Corps—an organization that helps communities around the world—and became a medical officer in West Africa. Being responsible for the health of two hundred people, far away from home, would prepare her for any challenge.

Mae returned to America to work as a doctor, but she had not forgotten her childhood dream. She learned everything she could about space travel, then contacted NASA to ask for an application form to join their space program. In 1987, after many grueling tests, she was selected as one of just fifteen candidates chosen from two thousand applicants.

Mae's dance training proved extremely useful. "To be a dancer, you have to be disciplined," she later explained. "You have to constantly rehearse and pay attention to other people; you have to memorize complicated routines and scenarios, and you have to be able to accept criticism and learn from it." On September 12, 1992 she put on her spacesuit and boarded the space shuttle *Endeavour*.

Dancing in orbit. On September 12, 1992, doctor and dancer Mae became the first African American woman in space.

Superstar. Aboard the space shuttle *Endeavour*, Mae completed 126 orbits around the Earth.

Mae circled the Earth 126 times and became the first African American woman to go into space. As mission specialist during her voyage she conducted several experiments, including two bone cell research studies, one on herself and the other on her fellow crew members.

She left NASA the following year, started a science camp for high school students and formed her own company, the Jemison Group, which encourages a love of science in students. She is also leader of the 100 Year Starship program, which is working towards making human space travel possible beyond the solar system.

Some think that space is something far away, that it is separate from us. Mae says, "I want you to go outside and look up, because you are looking into space and infinity ... I felt connected with the entire universe when I was in space, and I feel that connection now. I hope one day you'll look up and [feel] that as well."

GREENLAND

Josephine Peary explored the Arctic on a polar expedition, setting up camp in Greenland

ARCTIC OCEAN

Sacagawea helped European settlers navigate their way from Idaho to the Pacific coast via the Bitteroot Mountains

U.K.
Kent
BELGIUM
FRANCE
EUROPE

NORTH AMERICA

Mae Jemison grew up in Chicago and traveled into space with NASA

Bitteroot Mountains

U.S.

Chicago

New York

Nellie Bly traveled around the world in 72 days from New York

Sahara Desert

ATLANTIC OCEAN

AFRICA

PACIFIC OCEAN

SURINAME

Paramaribo

Galápagos Islands

ECUADOR

Alexandrine Tinné raced to find the source of the Nile River and made attempts to cross the Sahara Desert

TAHITI

Sylvia Earle explored the ocean floor and studied marine life in the Galápagos Islands in Ecuador

SOUTH AMERICA

Maria Sibylla Merian left her home in the Netherlands to study insects in Suriname

Jeanne Baret sailed around the globe, from France to Tahiti, to collect rare plant species

Junko Tabei climbed the world's highest peaks including Mount Everest in the Himalayas and Mount Nasu in Japan

Isabella Bird ventured from the U.K. to China to photograph and write about life on the Yangtze River

ASIA

Alborz Mountains

IRAN

EGYPT
Nile River

CHINA

TIBET
Lhasa

NEPAL

Mount Everest

JAPAN

Mount Nasu

Yangtze River

Alexandra David-Néel went on a pilgrimage from France to the city of Lhasa, Tibet

SINGAPORE

Freya Stark left Italy to re-map Iran's remote Alborz Mountains

PACIFIC OCEAN

INDIAN OCEAN

AUSTRALIA

OCEANIA

Auckland

Marianne North painted plants in the wild throughout Southeast Asia, including pitcher plants in Singapore

Jean Batten flew solo from Kent in the U.K. to Auckland, New Zealand

NEW ZEALAND

Hall of Fame

MARIA SIBYLLA MERIAN
1647–1717
Germany

Maria Sibylla Merian was an acclaimed naturalist and artist whose detailed observations of butterflies changed the way scientists studied insects forever. Over her life, she detailed the cycles of 186 insects and discovered many unknown species on her voyages. Her book *Metamorphosis Insectorum Surinamensium* is one of the most important books on natural history.

JEANNE BARET
1740–1807
France

Jeanne Baret was a French botanist who collected and catalogued over 6,000 species of plants. In 1775, she unknowingly became the first woman to sail around the world as part of the first French circumnavigation of the globe. In 2012, a new plant was named in her honor, the *Solanum baretiae.*

SACAGAWEA
1788–1812
U.S.

Sacagawea's achievements have become a symbol of strength and independence for women across America. Sacagawea was a guide and interpreter for the Lewis and Clark expedition, which traveled thousands of miles west across the American wilderness. Her bravery, skills with local plants, and quick thinking made her a valuable member of the expedition.

MARIANNE NORTH
1830–1890
U.K.

Marianne North was a Victorian botanical artist and biologist. Her impressive dedication to drawing plants and wildlife in their natural habitats saw her create over 800 striking paintings and discovering several new plant species. Today, her collection of stunning artwork can be seen at Kew Gardens, London.

ISABELLA BIRD
1831–1904
U.K.

Isabella Bird's extraordinary travels at the end of the nineteenth century were made famous through her writing and photography. Bird's accounts of the places she visited often challenged Western ideas of the time. She circumnavigated the world three times and became the first woman to be elected a Fellow at the Royal Geographical Society.

ALEXANDRINE TINNÉ
1835–1869
The Netherlands

Alexandrine Tinné made her mark by daring to be different. She challenged societal expectations of women and their place in the world of exploration. Born into money, Tinné used her wealth to fund expeditions into Sudan and Egypt. She died on her travels at the age of thirty-three from a knife wound.

JOSEPHINE PEARY
1863–1955
U.S.

Josephine Peary was an Arctic explorer whose book *My Arctic Journal* revealed the wonders and hardships of living in the High Arctic. In 1891, she became the first Western woman to take part in a polar expedition. She returned to the Arctic many times. In 1955 she was awarded the Medal of Achievement by the National Geographic Society.

NELLIE BLY
1864–1922
U.S.

Nellie Bly was a social activist and journalist whose creative and daring style of investigative reporting gained her huge popularity. She is famous for revealing the terrible conditions in a women's asylum in America and for her record-breaking journey in which she circled the globe in seventy-two days.

ALEXANDRA DAVID-NÉEL
1868-1969
France

Alexandra David-Néel was renowned for scaling the Himalayan peaks on foot to explore the Forbidden City of Lhasa in Tibet. She was a Buddhist follower and wrote over thirty books about her travels and eastern philosophy. Her writing inspired a generation of writers including the world-famous Jack Kerouac.

FREYA STARK
1893–1993
U.K./Italy

Writer and explorer Freya Stark was celebrated for her exploration of remote areas of Turkey, Asia and the Middle East, where few Europeans had traveled before. Her best-selling books combined practical travel tips with entertaining commentaries on the history and customs of the people and places she encountered. She was made Dame Commander of the British Empire in 1972.

JEAN BATTEN
1909–1982
New Zealand

Jean Batten was a record-breaking pilot and a fearless aviator. She flew several long-distance solo trips, including becoming the first person to fly solo from England to New Zealand in 1936. She won the Harmony Trophy for Outstanding Aviators three times.

SYLVIA EARLE
1935–present
U.S.

Sylvia Earle is a marine biologist and underwater explorer. Her innovative research and feats of exploration have led the way in advocating the protection of Earth's oceans and the environment. Her pioneering work in the study of marine life has helped change the way we understand our oceans.

JUNKO TABEI
1939–2016
Japan

Junko Tabei was a mountaineer whose passion and skill in climbing helped open up the world of mountaineering to women. She was the first woman to scale Mount Everest as well as all the highest peaks in the seven continents. Tabei became a leader for good environmental practice on the mountains.

MAE JEMISON
1956–present
U.S.

Mae Jemison is a scientist, doctor and astronaut. In 1992 she became the first African American woman to go into space aboard NASA's *Endeavour* space craft. Jemison is also celebrated for championing equal opportunities across the sciences and innovative technology. She is founder of the Jemison Group, and an international science camp for kids.

Glossary

BIOLUMINESCENCE the light that is produced by living organisms.

BOTANIST an expert in the study of plant life.

CABLEGRAM a message sent by an underwater cable.

CARAVAN a group of people traveling together across a desert.

COLONY a group of people from one country who build and occupy a settlement in another territory and claim the new land for their home nation.

COMPATRIOTS fellow citizens of a country.

DAME the female equivalent of receiving a knighthood by the Queen of the United Kingdom.

DYSENTERY an infectious disease of the digestive system.

ECOLOGY the study of living things, the environment and how they interact.

ECOSYSTEM is made up of all living and non-living things in an area.

EXPEDITION a group of people traveling for exploration.

FLORA all plants of a particular region, habitat, or geological period.

GEISHAS Japanese women who entertain through performing the ancient traditions of art, dance and singing. They wear kimonos and wear distinctive oshiroi makeup.

HOT SPRING a spring produced by hot groundwater that rises from the Earth's crust.

MALARIA a disease that is spread by the bite of a mosquito, which causes chills and fever.

METAMORPHOSIS the process of transformation or physical change. This happens in an insect or amphibian in two or more distinct stages, from a young form to an adult form.

NASA the National Aeronautics and Space Administration—an independent agency in the U.S., responsible for the American space program, as well as aeronautics and aerospace research.

NATURALIST an expert in the study of natural history.

ORBIT the path that an object, like a spacecraft, takes in space when it goes around a star, a planet, or a moon.

PEN NAME a made-up name, used by a writer instead of their real name.

PILGRIMAGE a journey to a holy place, often somewhere far away, for religious or spiritual reasons. Someone who makes a journey like this is a pilgrim.

RICKSHAWS small carts in India, pulled by men or women.

SCURVY a disease caused by a deficiency of vitamin C, which is found in fresh fruit, vegetables and meat. Sailors in the eighteenth and nineteenth centuries often suffered with scurvy on long sea voyages.

SPECIMEN a sample of something. Biologists collect specimens so they can study them closely.

SUBMERSIBLE a small submarine.

WILL a legal document in which a person expresses their wishes about how their property and belongings are to be shared after their death.

Copyright Credits

Images are listed by page number. Dimensions are given in cm (inches); height before width.

13 Maria Sibylla Merian, *Bananas and blue lizard*. From Maria Sibylla Merian, *Metamorphosis Insectorum Surinamensium*, Amsterdam, 1705. Smithsonian Libraries, Washington, D.C.

15 Maria Sibylla Merian, *Caterpillars, butterflies and flowers of a Palisade tree*. From Maria Sibylla Merian, *Metamorphosis Insectorum Surinamensium*, Amsterdam, 1719. Kunstmuseum Basel

17 Dorothea Maria Graff (attrib.), *Caiman wrestling with a red and black snake*, from an album entitled "Merian's Drawings of Surinam Insects &c," 1701–1705. Watercolor and bodycolor, heightened with white, and with pen and black ink, on vellum, 30.6 x 45.4 (12 1/16 x 17 7/8). Trustees of the British Museum, London

19 Maria Sibylla Merian, *Ripe pineapple with butterflies*. From Maria Sibylla Merian, *Metamorphosis Insectorum Surinamensium*, Amsterdam, 1705. Smithsonian Libraries, Washington, D.C.

25 Jeanne Baret. From James Cook, *Navigazioni di Cook pel grande oceano e intorno al globo...*, Milan, 1816–1817. State Library of New South Wales, Sydney (FL3740703)

26 Louis-Antoine de Bougainville, *Tahiti, the 'island of love'. View of New Cythera*, 1768. Watercolor drawing, 13 x 21 (5 1/8 x 8 3/8). Bibliothèque nationale de France, Paris

31 Edgar S. Paxson, *Lewis and Clark at Three Forks* (detail), 1912. Oil on canvas, 205.7 x 388.6 (81 x 153). Mural at the Montana State Capitol, Helena. Courtesy the Montana Historical Society (X1912.07.01)

32–33 Charles M. Russell, *Lewis and Clark on the Lower Columbia*, 1905. Opaque and transparent watercolor over graphite underdrawing on paper, 47.6 x 60.6 (18 3/4 x 23 7/8). Amon Carter Museum of American Art, Fort Worth, Texas, Amon G. Carter Collection, 1961.195

35a Sacagawea postage stamp, 28 July, 1954. Photo Granger Historical Picture Archive/ Alamy Stock Photo

35b Sacagawea with her child depicted on the U.S. Sacagawea dollar, 2000. Diam. 2.65 (1 1/8). Photo VPC Coins Collection/Alamy Stock Photo

39 Marianne North, *The Blue Puya and Cactus at Home in the Cordilleras, near Apogquindo, Chili*, 1880s. Oil on board, 35 x 51 (13 7/8 x 20 1/8). The Board of Trustees of the Royal Botanic Gardens, Kew

40 Julia Margaret Cameron, *Marianne North at her easel, Grahamstown, South Africa*, c. 1883. The Board of Trustees of the Royal Botanic Gardens, Kew

43 Marianne North, *A New Pitcher Plant from the Limestone Mountains of Sarawak*, 1876. Oil on board, 50.4 x 34.8 (19 7/8 x 13 3/4). The Board of Trustees of the Royal Botanic Gardens, Kew

47 Isabella Bird in riding dress. Title page illustration from Isabella L. Bird, *A Lady's Life in the Rocky Mountains*, London, 1879

48–49 Isabella Bird's houseboat on the Yangtze River at Kuei Fu. Photo by Isabella Bird, c. 1894–1896. John Murray Archive, National Library of Scotland, Edinburgh (MS.42033)

50 The Temple of the God of Literature at Mukden, capital of Manchuria. Hand-coloured lantern slide of a photo by Isabella Bird, c. 1894–1896. Hillier Collection, Royal Geographical Society via Getty Images

51 Isabella at her desk. Photo by Elliot & Fry, 1890s. Frontispiece to Anna M. Stoddart, *The Life of Isabella Bird (Mrs Bishop)*, London, 1906. Wellcome Library, London

55 Henri Auguste d'Ainecy (comte de) Montpézat, *Alexandrine Tinné*, 1849. Oil on canvas, 130 x 116 (51¼ x 45¾). Courtesy Haags Historisch Museum, The Hague

56 Alexandrine Tinné, *View of Tuti Island - Khartoum*, 1862–1863. Watercolor, 19 x 28.5 (7½ x 11¼). Courtesy Haags Historisch Museum, The Hague

57 Alexandrine Tinné, *Encampment in Desert*, 1862–1863. Watercolor, 19 x 28.5 (7½ x 11¼). Courtesy Haags Historisch Museum, The Hague

63 Mr. and Mrs. Peary on deck of "Roosevelt," Sydney. Photo Bain News Service, 1909. Library of Congress Prints and Photographs Division, Washington, D.C. (LC-DIG-ggbain-04265)

65 "Snowshoes," Josephine Peary in Northwest Greenland. Courtesy Herbert Collection

66 "Snow Baby." Courtesy Herbert Collection

67 "An Arctic Promenade - Mr. and Mrs. Peary on snowshoes." Courtesy Herbert Collection

69 Josephine and Marie Peary at Ellesmere Island base camp, 1901. Courtesy Herbert Collection

75 Nellie Bly, 1890. Library of Congress Prints and Photographs Division, Washington, D.C. (LC-USZ62-59924)

77 "Around the world in seventy-two days and six hours - reception of Nellie Bly at Jersey City on the completion of her journey," 1890. Includes two vignettes titled: "Presenting the Globe-Girdler a Golden Globe" and "The Arrival in Philadelphia." From sketches by C. Bunnell. Published in Frank Leslie's Illustrated Newspaper, vol. 70, no. 1795 (February 8, 1890). Library of Congress Prints and Photographs Division, Washington, D.C. (LC-USZ61-2126)

81 Alexandra and Yongden in northern Tibet, c. 1920–1923. Maison A. David-Néel, Digne-les-Bains. Alexandra David-Néel © Ville de Digne-les-Bains

82–83 Alexandra, Yongden (far left), and the Maharaja of Sikkim, Sidkeong Tulku (arms crossed), and various others, at Tangshung Pass, Sikkim, September 1914. Maison A. David-Neel, Digne-les-Bains. Alexandra David-Néel © Ville de Digne-les-Bains

85 Alexandra with nuns from the Chöten Nyma Monastery, Tibet, 1914. Maison A. David-Néel, Digne-les-Bains. Alexandra David-Néel © Ville de Digne-les-Bains

89 Wadi Hadhramaut caravan. Photo by Freya Stark, 1935. Royal Geographical Society/Alamy Stock Photo

90–91 Freya Stark in Jabal al-Druze, Syrian Arab Republic, 1928. Royal Geographical Society via Getty Images

93 British stamp from the "Extreme Endeavours" commemorative set, 2003, using a portrait of Freya Stark. Photo Sergey Goryachev/Shutterstock

97 Jean Gardner Batten, Rongotai Airport, Wellington. Unidentified photographer, c. 1936. Alexander Turnbull Library, Wellington, New Zealand (PAColl-0889-1)

99 Jean Gardner Batten in flying clothes alongside her airplane. Unidentified photographer, c. 1934. Alexander Turnbull Library, Wellington, New Zealand (1/2-046051-F)

100 Guide Bella and Jean Batten greeting each other with a hongi. Photo Moore and Thompson, c. 1936-1937, probably in the Rotorua district. Alexander Turnbull Library, Wellington, New Zealand (PAColl-8892)

105 Sylvia Earle prepares to dive in a JIM suit, 1979. Photo OAR/National Undersea Research Program (NURP)

107 Sylvia Earle below the surface on the Tektite II mission, St. John in the Virgin Islands, July, 1970. Photo AP/Shutterstock

108–109 Sylvia Earle investigates a towering tube sponge in Bonaire, the Caribbean. Photo David Doubilet/National Geographic

113 Junko Tabei and Ang Tshering against the background of the southern wall of Mount Everest, May, 1975. Photo Bettmann Archive/Getty Images

115 Junko Tabei on the summit of Mount Everest, 16 May 1975. Photo Tabei Kikaku Co Ltd/AP/Shutterstock

116 Junko Tabei, October, 1992. Photo John van Hasselt/Corbis via Getty Images

122–123 Mae Jemison works in the Spacelab Japan (SLJ) module aboard OV-105, September 1992. Photo NASA

124 Official portrait of astronaut candidate Mae C. Jemison. Photo taken October 1987. Photo NASA

Acknowledgements

My exploring life started early when my mum and dad took me to live in the Arctic. It was an experience that shaped and influenced everything that followed. So my greatest thanks go to my wise, loving and courageous mum and my much-missed, beloved dad; both of whom opened my eyes to the wonders of the natural world and encouraged me to open my heart to the extraordinary people we met along the way. Thanks always too to my closest friends for keeping me going, whatever the circumstances (you know who you are)! Thank you too to Anna Ridley and Sophy Thompson at Thames & Hudson for your faith and enthusiasm in my books, and thanks to my editor Harriet Birkinshaw and designer Belinda Webster for helping make these stories and pictures sing. And, of course, my love and thanks go to my biggest champions, Huw and Nell. I can't wait for our next adventure together.

Bibliography

JEAN BARET

Lewis-Jones, Huw. *Sea Journal.*
London: Thames & Hudson, 2019.

Ridley, Glynis. *The Discovery of
Jeanne Baret.* London: Random
House, 2011.

JEAN BATTEN

Batten, Jean. *My Life.* London:
Trotamundas Press, 2001.

Mackersey, Ian. *Jean Batten: The
Garbo of the Skies.* Auckland:
David Bateman Ltd, 2013.

ISABELLA BIRD

Bird, Isabella. *A Lady's Life in the
Rocky Mountains.* London: Putnum
& Sons, 1879.

Ireland, Debbie. *Isabella Bird:
A Photographic Journal of Travels
through China.* London: Ammonite
Press, 2015.

NELLIE BLY

Bly, Nellie. *Around the World in 72
Days: And Other Writings.* London:
Penguin Classics, 2014.

Christensen, Bonnie. *The Daring
Nellie Bly: America's Star Reporter.*
London: Dragonfly Books, 2009

ALEXANDRA DAVID-NÉEL

David-Néel, Alexandra. *My Journey
to Lhasa.* London: Harper
Perennial, 2008.

Middleton, Ruth. *Alexandra David-
Néel: Portrait of an Adventurer.*
London: Shambhala, 1989.

SYLVIA EARLE

Earle, Sylvia. *Blue Hope: Exploring
and Caring for Earth's Magnificent
Ocean.* Washington D.C.: National
Geographic, 2014.

Nivola, Claire. *Life in the Ocean: The
Story of Oceanographer Sylvia
Earle.* New York: Macmillan, 2012.

MAE JEMISON

Jemison, Mae. *Find Where the Wind
Goes: Moments From my Life.*
New York: Scholastic, 2001.

Pincus, Meeg. *Mae C, Jemison.* New
York: Discovery Library, 2019.

MARIA SIBYLLA MERIAN

Pomeroy, Sarah. *Maria Sibylla
Merian: Artist, Scientist, Adventurer.*
London: Getty Publications, 2018.

Sidman, Joyce. *The Girl Who Drew
Butterflies.* London: HMH Books for
Young Readers, 2018.

MARIANNE NORTH

North, Marianne. *Abundant Beauty:
    The Adventurous Travels of
    Marianne North, Botanical Artist*.
    Toronto: Greystone Books, 2010.
Payne, Michelle. *Marianne North:
    A Very Intrepid Painter*. London:
    Kew Publishing, 2011.

JOSEPHINE PEARY

Herbert, Kari. *Heart of the Hero:
    The Remarkable Women who
    Inspired the Great Polar Explorers*.
    Glasgow: Saraband Books, 2013.
Peary, Josephine, *My Arctic Journal*.
    New York: Cooper Square Press,
    2002.

SACAGAWEA

Jazynka, Kitson. *National Geographic
    Readers: Sacagawea*. New York:
    National Geographic, 2015.
Lohnes Frazier, Net., *Path to the
    Pacific: The Story of Sacagawea*.
    Minnesota: Young Yoyageur, 2016.

FREYA STARK

Geniesse, Jane Fletcher. *Passionate
    Nomad: The Life of Freya Stark*.
    New York: Modern Library, 2001.
Stark, Freya. *Traveller's Prelude:
    Autobiography, 1893-1927*. London:
    Arrow Books, 1989.

JUNKO TABEI

McLoone, Margo. *Women Explorers
    of the Mountains*. New York:
    Capstone, 1999.
Tabei, Junko. *Honouring High Places:
    The Mountain Life of Junko Tabei*.
    Calgary: Rocky Mountain Books,
    2017.

ALEXANDRINE TINNÉ

Herbert, Kari and Lewis-Jones, Huw.
    *Explorers' Sketchbooks: The Art of
    Discovery and Adventure*. London:
    Thames & Hudson 2017.
Willink, Robert Joost. *The Fateful
    Journey: The Expedition of Alexine
    Tinné and Theodor Von Heuglin in
    Sudan (1863-1864)*. Amsterdam:
    Amsterdam University Press, 2011.

About the Author

KARI HERBERT first started traveling at the age of ten months when her parents, author Marie and polar explorer Wally, took her to the Arctic. For two years the family lived with a small tribe of Inuit on a remote island off the coast of Northwest Greenland. Kari has continued to travel extensively ever since. She has written several books on exploration, women's history and visual culture; her most recent being *Explorers' Sketchbooks*, co-authored with her husband Huw Lewis-Jones, and *We Are Artists*. When she's not exploring wild and woolly places, Kari can be found by the sea in Cornwall where she lives with Huw and their adventurous daughter Nell.

Kari and her father Sir Wally Herbert in northwest Greenland, 1972.

Index

First published in the United States of America in 2021 by
Thames & Hudson Inc., 500 Fifth Avenue, New York, New York 10110

We Are Explorers © 2021 Thames & Hudson Ltd, London

Text and original illustrations © 2021 Kari Herbert
Reproductions see pp. 137–139

Edited by AHA Editorial
Designed by Belinda Webster

All Rights Reserved. No part of this publication may be reproduced or
transmitted in any form or by any means, electronic or mechanical,
including photocopy, recording or any other information storage and
retrieval system, without prior permission in writing from the publisher.

Library of Congress Control Number 2020940144

ISBN 978-0-500-65239-8

Printed in Singapore by 1010 Printing International Ltd

Be the first to know about our new releases,
exclusive content and author events by visiting
thamesandhudson.com
thamesandhudsonusa.com
thamesandhudson.com.au